The Tale of Two Athletes:
The Story of Jumper and The Thumper

Workbook:

Steps to Tackle Childhood Obesity

By Jeana R. Griffith, Ph.D.

AuthorHouse™
1663 Liberty Drive
Bloomington, IN 47403
www.authorhouse.com
Phone: 1-800-839-8640

Published by AuthorHouse 7/20/2012

ISBN: 978-1-4772-4534-7 (e)
ISBN: 978-1-4772-4086-1 (sc)

About the Author

Jeana R. Griffith, Ph.D. is a licensed Clinical Psychologist. She is a graduate of Miami University in Oxford, Ohio. She did her internship and Post- Doctoral studies at Emory University School of Medicine in Atlanta, Georgia. Dr. Jeana R. Griffith is a former Assistant Professor at Emory University School of Medicine. She is currently a psychotherapist at Georgia State University Counseling and Testing Center in Atlanta, Georgia. She also serves as an Adjunct professor for Emory University School of Medicine, is the Coordinator for the Rainbows Program (a support group for children who have experienced a loss), and teaches Religious Education Classes at her church.

Dr. Jeana R. Griffith is committed to helping underserved populations and those with chronic illnesses. She has conducted research and has publications in the areas of sickle cell disease, depression, and weight, shape, and eating in African Americans. She enjoys community outreach and has given presentations on various topics including: Childhood Obesity, Bullying, Coping with Loss, Overcoming Joy Blockers, and Depression in the Cancer Patient. Dr. Griffith is also a team leader for Georgia's Walk for Lupus Now an Annual fundraising walk for The Lupus Foundation.

Over the past several years, Dr. Jeana R. Griffith has joined with her husband M. Christopher Griffith, M.D. in the fight against childhood obesity. They have co-authored the book <u>The Tale of Two Athletes: The Story of Jumper and The Thumper: Understanding and Combating Childhood Obesity</u> to inspire children and their families to live a healthier life style. They travel around the country telling the story and changing lives.

Dr. Griffith resides in Lithonia, Georgia with her husband and two children.

Dedication

This book is dedicated to my amazing husband. Thanks for all of your support throughout the years. I hope this workbook helps you with your mission in the fight against childhood obesity.

Table of Contents

A Note From the Author

<u>To Children:</u> Join Jasmine on her journey to a healthier lifestyle. As you read this book and are inspired to live a healthier lifestyle, remember that every day is a new day. Each morning when you wake up you have a choice between living a healthy lifestyle or living an unhealthy lifestyle. Remember YOU have the power to choose. Change takes education, focus, work/practice, and a positive attitude. It isn't always easy to make a change in your life but remember anything worth having is usually worth the effort. Visualize your goal, focus on it, and then go to work. If you visualize yourself being successful then you will be more likely to do the steps necessary to reach your goal. As you work through the exercises and games in this workbook, you are becoming one of the characters in the story: *The Tale of Two Athletes: The Story of Jumper and The Thumper*. How will your story end?... May you have a Happy Ending!

<u>To Parents/Guardians:</u> This workbook is intended for children ages 9-12 and their parents. The goal is the development of a healthier lifestyle, as opposed to the overly thin "ideal body type" as portrayed in some media images. This workbook will help you and your family begin by taking small steps toward health. As parents it is important to help your child (along with your healthcare providers' advice) set realistic goals for themselves and maintain a positive, upbeat approach to achieving them. Developing a healthier lifestyle is best achieved if it is a "family goal" rather than an individual child's goal. Parents can model for their child appropriate eating and exercise habits. There are many websites available that have information about childhood obesity. These websites contain valuable information that may help you and your family achieve your goals. Information such as: diet and physical activity guidelines, games, suggested meal plans, and further suggested readings. Some of these websites are listed at the end of this workbook. It is also important to meet with your child's healthcare provider to determine healthy weight goals for your child, suggestions for proper nutrition, and exercise recommendations. Parents/guardians are encouraged to visit our Facebook page: www.Facebook.com/JumperandTheThumper. Here you and your child can sign in and become one of the characters in the fight against childhood obesity.

-Jeana R. Griffith, Ph.D.

***

*<u>Note:</u> This workbook is a tool to help families get started on the road to a healthier lifestyle. The information contained in this book is intended to complement not replace the advice of your healthcare provider. Consult with your healthcare provider before beginning any program. He/She can discuss your child's individual needs and counsel you about symptoms and treatment. If you have any questions regarding how the material in this workbook applies to your child, then speak with your healthcare provider.

Introduction

The book, *The Tale of Two Athletes: The Story of Jumper and The Thumper,* by M.Christopher Griffith, M.D. and Jeana R. Griffith, Ph.D. (2012) is inspiring children and their families to be healthier. As parents/guardians we can help guide our children toward a healthier life style one step at a time. We also can take advantage of making healthier choices for ourselves.

The *Dietary Guidelines for Americans 2010* identifies three major goals:

1. Balance calories with physical activity to manage weight.

2. Consume more of certain foods and nutrients such as fruits, vegetables, whole grains, fat-free and low fat dairy products, and seafood.

3. Consume fewer foods with sodium (salt), saturated fats, trans fats, cholesterol, added sugars, and refined grains.

This workbook will help you and your child/children achieve these goals. It uses the characters Jasmine, Jumper, and The Thumper from *The Tale of Two Athletes: The Story of Jumper and The Thumper* to take children and their caregivers on a journey toward a healthier lifestyle. It is made up of 5 sections:

Part One: Telling Your Story - This section helps children tell their story about being overweight and its impact upon their lives. Children are helped to identify their feelings about being overweight, ways of coping with being teased/bullied, and use diaries to help identify their current eating and activity patterns.

Part Two: Making Changes - In this section, children and their caregivers are empowered and educated to begin making changes in their lives. They are empowered in their visit to their healthcare provider through useful questions to ask their doctor. They are educated about healthy food alternatives, how to read product labels, slowing down to enjoy their food, physical activity requirements for children, and the recommended daily requirements for the five food groups. These lessons are supplemented with games and fun activities to involve the family.

Part Three: Steps to a Healthier You - In this section, children and their caregivers (following their healthcare provider's recommendations) make an individualized plan for achieving a healthier lifestyle, set small steps to achieve their overall goals for eating and exercise, visualize success, and use positive self- affirmations to help keep them motivated. Children use food and activity diaries, a weekly caregiver check-in to monitor their progress, and are rewarded for their success.

Part Four: Handling Setbacks/Staying With It - In this section, children identify potential bumps in their road to a healthier lifestyle and ways to cope/overcome them. Children are also encouraged to stay with their new healthier lifestyle through useful tips and suggestions.

Part Five: Celebrating a Healthier You - In this section, children decorate and receive their workbook completion certificate and name their character for the story. They then tell their story in words or pictures about their journey to a healthier lifestyle. Children, along with their caregivers' assistance, are encouraged to visit Facebook and "Like" the Jumper and The Thumper page, where they can share the name of their new character, interact with the authors, and learn more about their efforts to inspire families to be healthier.

This workbook encourages children and their families to take small steps toward the larger goal of being healthier. It is acknowledged that change does not occur overnight and it requires patience and a change in attitude and behaviors. This is not to say that you can never go to your favorite fast food restaurant or ever have ice cream. Remember, moderation is the key to living healthier.

__Note:__ This book is not intended to take the place of medical advice. Seek your healthcare provider's advice about the best plan to help in your fight against childhood obesity.

Due to the nature of the internet, the websites listed in this book may have changed since publication and may no longer be valid.

Key Terms

Body Mass Index (BMI)- a number calculated from a person's height and weight. It is a screening tool used to identify possible weight problems. The BMI is used along with other measures (such as assessment of medical history, family history, physical activity, diet, and laboratory tests) to determine if a child is overweight. Visit http://apps.nccd.cdc.gov/dnpabmi/ for a child and adolescent BMI calculator.

BMI for Age Percentile- the BMI is plotted on growth charts to arrive at a percentile used to compare a child's weight to other children their same sex and age.

Empty Calories- these are calories from solid fats and added sugars. Avoid foods/drinks with a lot of empty calories.

Healthy Weight- a range of weight that is considered healthy for a given height. In children and teens it is the 5th percentile to less than the 85th percentile (BMI for age percentile).

Overweight- a range of weight that is considered unhealthy for a given height. In children and teens it is the 85th percentile to less than the 95th percentile (BMI for age percentile).

Obese- a range of weight that is considered very unhealthy for a given height. In children and teens it is equal to or greater than the 95th percentile (BMI for age percentile).

%DV= % Daily Value. This is the percentage of daily required nutrients provided by the food product. It is found on the product label.

Saturated Fats- are solid fats such as butter. These are considered "bad fats" and should be limited in a persons' diet.

Trans Fats- are a type of solid fat. Partially hydrogenated oils such as stick margarine contain trans fats. These are considered "bad fats" and should be limited in a person's diet.

Monounsaturated Fat- most of the daily recommended fats consumed should be this type. They are fats that are liquid at room temperature and start to become solid when chilled. An example is olive oil.

Polyunsaturated Fat- most of the daily recommended fats consumed should be this type. They are fats that are liquid at room temperature and when chilled. An example is safflower oil.

PART ONE:

Telling Your Story

Goals:

- Help children tell their story about being overweight and its impact on their lives.
- Help children identify and express their feelings about being overweight.
- Identify ways to cope with being teased or bullied for being overweight.
- Identify the child's current daily food and activity patterns.
- Identify the health risks associated with being overweight.

In the beginning of the story <u>The Tale of Two Athletes: The Story of Jumper and The Thumper,</u> the character Jasmine looked at herself in the mirror. When Jasmine looked in the mirror she saw a girl who was gaining weight. Her clothes were getting too tight. Her button had popped off her pants and she was sad.

When You Look in the Mirror
What Do You See?

(Write or draw your response in the mirror)

Jasmine told her story about how she was teased for being overweight. Kids called her names like "Factory Fat Girl". Now it is time to <u>Tell Your Story.</u>

How has Childhood Obesity or Being Overweight Affected Your Life?
(Draw or write your story below)

Jasmine had many feelings about being overweight she was <u>SAD</u> when her button popped off her pants, <u>**FRUSTRATED**</u> when she was trying to lose weight and the food kept calling her. The Thumper was <u>SCARED</u> and <u>MAD</u> when the bullies teased him, and he felt <u>LOVED</u> by mom when she hugged him.

What Feelings Do You Have About Being Overweight?

Circle **All** the Feelings you have. You may have more than one feeling:

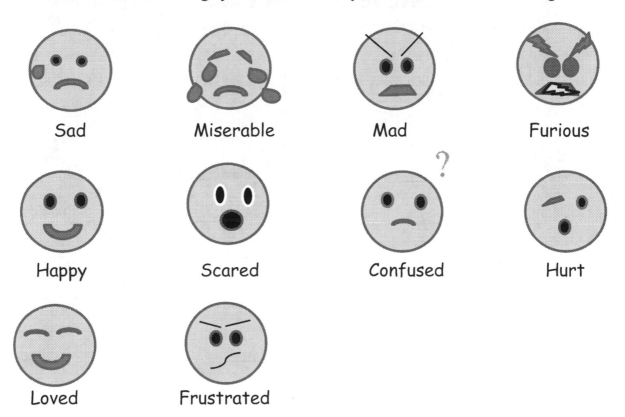

Sad   Miserable   Mad   Furious

Happy   Scared   Confused   Hurt

Loved   Frustrated

You Can Write or Draw More Feelings below:

Jasmine and Thumper were both teased for being overweight. These are the things they did to help them cope.

Coping with Being Teased/Bullied for Being Overweight

These are the things that Jasmine and The Thumper did to help them cope with being bullied/teased for being overweight:

(Circle the ones that you have tried or would like to try if you are being teased/ bullied)

Talk to a parent   Talk to a Counselor   Talk to a Teacher/Coach

Talk to a friend   Talk to a relative   Write about it in a journal

Write your own _____

_____

_____

Jasmine's typical day was to wake up at 7 a.m., wash, eat breakfast, go to school, eat lunch, come home, eat a snack, do her homework, eat dinner, watch T.V., eat a snack, play video games, eat a snack, and go to bed at 9:30 p.m.

Describe Your Typical Day

Time	Activity

How many activities involved exercise/movement? _____

How many activities involved mostly sitting? _____

My Food Diary

Day of the Week	Time of Day	What You Ate	How Much or How Many?

How many times did you eat between meals? _____

My Physical Activity Diary

Day of Week	Time of Day	Activity	Duration

Health Risk Coding Game

Can you decode the puzzle to unveil some of the health risks of being Overweight?

1 15 16 7 10 1

___ ___ ___ ___ ___ ___

7 8 6 7
3 7 12 9 5 15 16 5 14 12 9

___ ___ ___ ___

___ ___ ___ ___ ___ ___ ___ ___ ___ ___ ___

7 17 13 5 14 16 5 11 15 8 12 11

___ ___ ___ ___ ___ ___ ___ ___ ___ ___ ___ ___

4 8 1 2 5 16 5 15

___ ___ ___ ___ ___ ___ ___ ___

DECODER KEY								
1 = A	2 = B	3 = C	4 = D	5 = E	6 = G	7 = H	8 = I	9 = L
10 = M	11 = N	12 = O	13 = P	14 = R	15 = S	16 = T	17 = Y	

Answers: Health Risk Decoder Game

ASTHMA

HIGH CHOLESTEROL

HYPERTENSION (Also called High Blood Pressure)

DIABETES

PART TWO:

Making Changes
(Educate, Empower, and Change)

Goals:

- Empower the child and their parent/guardian as they attend a visit to their healthcare provider.
- Obtain the healthcare provider's assessment of the child's specific needs for weight loss and increased physical activity.
- Establish a weight loss/healthier lifestyle contract.
- Educate the family about healthy food choices and alternatives.
- Educate the family regarding food labels.
- Educate the family about the five food groups.
- Empower parents to make changes.
- Help children and their family slow down and enjoy their food.
- Educate the family about foods that satisfy a sweet tooth and foods that keep a person full longer.
- Educate the family about the relationship between physical activity and food intake as they relate to weight.
- Help children identify the types of physical activity they will try.
- Educate the family about recommended exercise requirements for children.
- Help the family see the relationship between exercise and improved mood and exercise and improved energy.

When Jasmine was upset about her button popping off her pants, she told her mother about it. Her mother took her to the doctor for a check- up.

The Check-up*
Some Questions to ask Your Doctor

1. How much do I weigh? _____

2. What is my body mass index? _____

3. How much weight do I need to lose to be healthier? _____

4. What suggestions does the doctor have for me to lose weight?

_____

_____

_____

5. What suggestions does my doctor have to help my family adopt a healthier eating and exercise lifestyle? _____

_____

_____

6. Do I have any exercise restrictions? _____

_____

7. Is it safe for me to begin a diet and exercise plan? _____

*<u>**Note:**</u> Take your Food and Activity Diaries with you to your appointment so your doctor can see your current eating patterns and activity level.

_____

Weight Loss/ Healthier Lifestyle Contract

I _____ would like to lose _____lbs.

My parent(s)/guardian(s)_____

agree to help me with this goal by being supportive and helping me to

make healthy food and exercise choices.

Signed _____

Parent/Guardian _____

Parent/Guardian _____

My Health Care Provider _____

*Note: Parents/guardians are also encouraged to set goals for themselves and other members of the family are encouraged to do so as well. Effective change occurs when everyone in the family is working together toward a common goal, e.g., a healthier lifestyle.

When Jasmine heard the story <u>The Tale of Two Athletes: The Story of Jumper and The Thumper,</u> she saw that Jumper exercised and ate healthy foods whereas The Thumper did not. Jumper was thin and lean and The Thumper was massive and overweight. Jasmine realized that she would have to make better food choices and exercise to lose weight and be healthier.

Foods to Avoid

<u>Rule:</u> *Keep these low. Look at the %DV (% Daily Value) on the product label. Anything 5% of DV or less is low and anything 20% of DV or more is high.*

Salty (high sodium) foods: such as chips, crackers, etc.
Saturated fats
Trans fats
High Cholesterol
Added Sugars
Refined Grains

Foods to Enjoy

<u>Rule:</u> *Get enough of these. Look at the %DV (% Daily Value) on the product label. Anything 5% of DV or less is low and anything 20% of DV or more is high. You want to make sure you get enough Potassium, Fiber, Vitamins A & C, Calcium, and Iron.*

Fruits
Vegetables
Whole grains
Fat-free dairy products
Low fat dairy products
Seafood

*Remember to also pay attention to the number of calories in a product and the serving size. Also remember fat free does not equal calorie free. Avoid high calorie foods and empty calories.

When Jasmine went to the store her mother showed her how to read the labels on food products.

Read the Labels Game

Help Jasmine Read the labels on foods and decide if it is a food to <u>enjoy</u> or a food to <u>avoid</u>. Remember if it does not have a label it is probably a fresh fruit or vegetable so ENJOY.

<u>Hint:</u> Look at the serving size first. How many servings per container? How many calories? Look at the % of Daily Value for fat, cholesterol, sodium, fiber, protein, sugar, vitamins, and minerals. *Anything 5% of DV or less is low and anything 20% of DV or more is high.*

Label #1:

Nutrition Facts

Serving Size: ½ cup
Servings per container: 2
Calories: 250   Calories from Fat: 110

	%Daily Value
Total Fat 15 g.	20%
Saturated	18%
Trans Fat	0%
Cholesterol	21%
Sodium 470mg.	20%
Potassium 0 g.	0%
Dietary Fiber 0 g.	0%
Sugar 5g.	0%
Protein 4 g.	0%
Vitamin A	2%
Vitamin C	4%
Calcium	20%
Iron	2%

Avoid ☐   or   Enjoy ☐
(Place a check in the box you think is correct)

Label #2:

Nutrition Facts	
Serving Size: ¼ cup dry	
Servings per container: 8	
Calories: 170 Calories from Fat: 15	

	%Daily Value
Total Fat 1.5 g.	2%
Saturated 0	0%
Trans Fat 0	0%
Cholesterol 0	0%
Sodium 0 mg.	0%
Potassium 100 g.	3%
Dietary Fiber 2 g.	8%
Sugar 0 g.	0%
Protein 4 g.	0%
Vitamin A	0 %
Vitamin C	0 %
Calcium	0%
Iron	2 %
Thiamin	10%
Folate	4%
Niacin	10%

Avoid ☐   or Enjoy ☐
(Place a check in the box you think is correct)

Label #3:

Nutrition Facts

Serving Size: 1 cup
Servings per container: 2
Calories: 290   Calories from Fat: 150

	% Daily Value
Total Fat 17 g.	26%
Saturated 7g.	34%
Trans Fat 1g.	0%
Cholesterol 85mg.	28%
Sodium 1190mg.	49%
Dietary Fiber 1g.	5%
Sugar 3g.	
Protein 26 g.	

Vit. A	25%
Vit. C	15%
Calcium	4%
Iron	20%

Avoid ☐   or   Enjoy ☐
(Place a check in the box you think is correct)

Answers: Read the Label Game

Label #1: Avoid- this product has high calories (500 calories if you eat the whole container), high fat, high sodium, and high cholesterol.

Label #2: Enjoy- this product is low in fat, has no sodium, has no sugar, and has no cholesterol.

Label #3: Avoid- although this product is a good source of Vitamin A and iron, this product has high calories, high fat (saturated fat), high sodium, and high cholesterol. The bad outweighs the good.

Dr. G. gave Jasmine a list of food alternatives to help her make better food choices. He told her that she could still eat the foods she loved, but in fat-free or low-calorie alternatives.

Food Alternatives

Adapted from http://www.nhlbi.nih.gov/health/public/heart/obesity/lose_wt/lcal_fat.htm.

Low-Calorie, Lower-Fat Alternative Foods.

Refer to this website for a more complete list.

Higher Fat Food	Lower Fat Alternative
Whole Milk	Low-fat (1%), Reduced Fat (2%) or Fat-Free (skim) milk
Ice Cream	Sorbet, low-fat or fat-free frozen yogurt or ice cream
Cheese	Fat-Free or reduced-calorie cheese
Sour Cream	Plain low-fat yogurt
Ramen Noodles	Rice or noodles (spaghetti, macaroni, etc.)
Pasta with white sauce	Pasta with red sauce
Granola	Reduced-fat granola, bran flakes, crispy rice, cooked grits or oatmeal
Lunch meat	Low-fat lunch meat (95-97% fat-free)
Hot dogs (regular)	Low-fat hot dogs
Bacon or sausage	Canadian Bacon or ham
Ground beef (regular)	Extra-lean ground beef or ground turkey. Soy burgers.
Chicken or Turkey with skin	Chicken or Turkey without skin
Frozen breaded fish	Fish or shellfish, unbreaded (fresh frozen, canned in water)
Whole eggs	Egg whites
Frozen T.V. dinner with 13 grams of fat per serving	Frozen T.V. dinner with less than 13 grams of fat per serving and lower in sodium
Croissants	Hard French rolls or soft brown 'n' serve rolls
Donuts, sweet rolls, muffins	English muffins, bagels, reduced-fat or fat-free muffins
Cake	Cake (Angel food, white or gingerbread)
Cookies	Reduced-fat or fat-free cookies (graham crackers, ginger snaps, fig bars) Choose the lowest calorie variety
Nuts	Popcorn (air popped or light microwave), fruits, vegetables
Regular mayonnaise	Light mayonnaise
Oils, shortening, or lard	Nonstick cooking spray for stir-frying or sautéing Instead of oil or butter, use applesauce or prune puree in baked goods.
Avocado on sandwiches	Cucumber or lettuce leaves
Canned cream soups	Canned broth based soups
Guacamole dip or refried beans with lard	Salsa

Even with this food list Jasmine still missed her chocolate bars. She went to see Dr. G. He told her that she could still have chocolate bars but she should eat them less often or eat a smaller version. He told her that if she added exercise it would help her to burn the calories.

Dr. G. Weight loss Tips:

- You can still enjoy the foods you love. Just eat a smaller portion or eat them less often. For example instead of a candy bar each day, eat a candy bar once a week.

- Increase physical activity- Balance what you take in with exercise to burn the calories. Take a walk, ride a bike, run, etc.

- Instead of sugary drinks like soda and sports drinks (which can have up to 10 teaspoons of sugar in them), drink water or sparkling water.

- Make half of your plate fruits and vegetables.

- Eat grilled or baked fish and chicken instead of fried.

- Eat baked sweet potato fries instead of French fried white potatoes.

- Eat more whole grains.

- Read the labels on food products at the store.

- Eat fat-free or low-fat products (be sure to check the calories on the label).

- Avoid fast food and take out instead make a meal at home with your family.

- Don't be fooled by the other names used for added sugars like: glucose, high-fructose corn syrup, corn syrup, maple syrup, agave nectar, sucrose, dextrose, and fructose. If one of these or sugar is one of the first three ingredients on a food label then avoid it.

- Don't keep those tempting "foods to avoid" in your house.

- Have fruits and veggies cut up and stored in your fridge for quick and easy snacking.

Jasmine like The Thumper loved sweets and hated feeling hungry. These foods helped satisfy her sweet tooth and/or kept her full longer.

Foods that Satisfy Sweet Tooth and/or Keep You Full Longer.
(Adapted from www.ivillage.com/Trying to Lose Weight? 50 Delicious (& Healthy) Foods and Drinks that Fill You Up)

- **Dark chocolate is more satisfying than milk chocolate.**

- **Whole grains stay with you longer than white flour products. Try whole grain cereal, crackers, and pasta.**

- **Drink a glass of fat free milk when you get hungry. Put a little chocolate syrup in the milk to help your sweet craving.**

- **Eat melons. They will help your sweet tooth and because they contain lots of water they will help you feel full.**

- **Air popped popcorn. (Jasmine likes putting hot sauce on her popcorn for a little extra kick, instead of butter or salt).**

- **Beans have protein and help keep you full. (Try pinto beans in chili. Jasmine's favorite).**

- **Greek yogurt has twice the protein of regular yogurt which keeps you satisfied longer.**

- **Try peanut butter instead of jelly.**

- **Oatmeal sweetened with fresh fruit. (Jasmine likes to use a little honey).**

Tip for Parents

Your child should eat a variety of foods from the 5 major food groups.
The food groups and daily allowance recommendations listed below are from the U.S. Department of Agriculture and the U.S. Department of Health and Human Services (adapted from Healthychildren.org):

Vegetables: 3-5 servings per day. A serving is 1 cup of raw leafy vegetables, ¾ cup of vegetable juice, or ½ cup of other vegetables (raw or cooked).

Fruits: 2-4 servings per day. A serving is ½ cup of sliced fruit, ¾ cup of fruit juice, or a medium size whole fruit (such as apple, banana, or pear).

Bread, Cereal, or Pasta: 6-11 servings per day. Each serving should equal 1 slice of bread, ½ cup of rice or pasta, or 1 ounce of cereal.

Protein Foods: 2-3 servings of 2-3 ounces of cooked lean meat, poultry, or fish per day. A serving can also consist of ½ cup cooked dry beans, one egg, or 2 tablespoons of peanut butter for each ounce of lean meat.

Dairy Products: 2-3 servings per day of 1 cup of low-fat milk or yogurt, or 1 ½ ounces of natural cheese.

Note: Although oils are not a food group, they provide essential nutrients for health such as vitamin E and essential fatty acids. The recommended daily allowance of oils for a child age 9-13 years is approximately 5 teaspoons. A person should consume the correct type of oils mostly (monounsaturated and polyunsaturated) and avoid saturated and Trans fat. Oils can come from nuts, salad dressing, mayonnaise, or cooking oil. Also, be mindful that 1tablespoon of oil has 120 calories.
(See www.choosemyplate.gov for more information on oils).

<u>Empowering Parents</u>

- Did you know that there are less fresh fruits and healthy food choices in low income neighborhoods? You can make a difference by requesting them. Some popular pharmacy food chains now have baskets of fresh fruit at their check out. Have your children grab an apple instead of that candy bar.

- Speak with your child's school to see if they have healthy food options for its students. Start a campaign to request healthy food alternatives and snacks for your child's school.

- Parents can save money and feel more empowered at the grocery store checkout if they buy fruits in season and buy whole fruits and vegetables as opposed to the more expensive pre-cut variety. (visit www.fruitsandveggiesmatter.gov for tips on how to stretch your fruit and vegetable budget).

- If you must eat out, help your children make smart food selections like baked or grilled chicken instead of fried, water instead of soda, and fruit instead of chocolate cake for dessert. Also, avoid all you can eat buffets and supersized items.

- Have picky eaters? Let your kids' help you shop and pick out new healthy foods to try. Kids are more likely to taste new things if they are involved in helping to pick it out and prepare it. Also, try cutting foods into fun shapes.

- Visit the websites in Appendix A for healthy recipe ideas, exercise charts, and child friendly healthy living interactive activities to help keep you and your family inspired.

One of Jasmine and The Thumpers' problems was that they both liked to eat their food really fast. Dr. G. taught Jasmine to slow down and enjoy her food. He told her to turn off the T.V., focus on her food, its taste, texture, color, and smell. Slowing down and enjoying her food enabled Jasmine to eat less.

Game

What Spice is in Your Food?

Purpose: To get family members to slow down and enjoy their food by noticing its different tastes, textures, colors, and smells.

How to Play: Parent/Guardian serves a dish with a variety of spices in it. Family members take turns guessing what is in the dish. Encourage them to notice its texture, look at its color, taste it and smell it. Whoever correctly guesses the most spices in the food is the winner.

*Tip: Try using spices with rich color such as curry and paprika. Also try spices with great taste and smell such as: cinnamon, curry, nutmeg, and rosemary.

In the story about Jumper and The Thumper, The Thumper took in more calories than he burned through exercise. Therefore, The Thumper was overweight. Whereas, Jumper took in fewer calories than he burned through exercise, therefore, Jumper was very thin.

Compare the Scales:

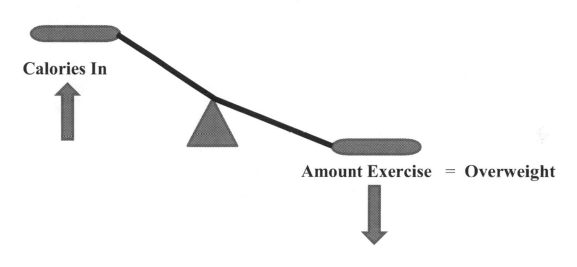

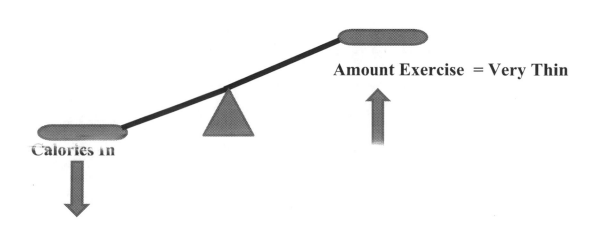

When Jasmine went to see Dr. G. he told her that children her age should do 60 minutes of physical activity per day. He also told her to limit the time she spends on the computer, watching T.V. or playing video games to 2 hours or less per day.

Circle the types of exercise you would like to try. Choose more than one so that you can vary what you do each day.

Bike riding	Gymnastics
Pull ups	Weight lifting
Running	Take a walk
Jumping rope	Jumping Jacks
Swimming	Tennis
Basketball	Baseball
Soccer	Volleyball
Dancing	Aerobics
Hiking	Write in: _____

For Parents:

<u>Did You Know?</u>

- Younger children like to move between different activities and do short bursts of activity followed by a rest break. Try a game of tag, or climbing on a jungle gym.
- Teenagers can do more structured activities for longer periods of time. Try a structured weight lifting program or running for longer periods (ask a doctor about the appropriate routine for your child's needs).
- Children tend to exercise more if they see their parents doing it.
- You can build physical activity into your daily routine. Start taking a walk together as a family after dinner, do yard or housework together, or dance to music together each evening.
- If you use a variety of different types of exercise in your routine, then you are less likely to get bored and stop exercising. Try biking one day then swimming another, etc.
- Most children love to learn new games. Try four square, Frisbee baseball (throw the Frisbee and run the bases), a scavenger hunt, or capture the flag.
- Exercise can burn calories, burn fat, reduce appetite, and reduce stress.
- Aerobic activity should make up most of a child's 60 minutes of physical activity each day. Children (ages 6-17 years) should do vigorous activities at least 3 days per week. An example is running or a brisk walk.
- Children (ages 6-17 years) should do muscle strengthening activities at least 3 days per week as part of their 60 minutes per day of exercise. An example is push-ups or gymnastics.
- Children (ages 6-17 years) should do bone strengthening activities at least 3 days per week as part of their 60 minutes per day of exercise. An example is jumping rope.

Dance to the Music Family Game:

<u>Purpose</u>: **to see how different types of music makes you feel and to see whether dancing improves mood and energy.**

1. Rate <u>How you Feel</u> on a scale from 0-10:

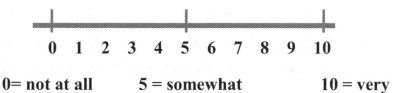

0= not at all   5 = somewhat   10 = very

Write a number in the spaces below for each feeling:

Happy _____   Sad _____   Full of Energy _____   Sluggish _____

2. Put on different types of music for 1 minute each (30 seconds for younger children).

For example: R & B, Rap, Rock, Heavy Metal, Classical, Latin, and Jazz.
Then start moving to the music. Notice how the beats are different and how the music makes you feel and move. For classical you may move like you are doing ballet, for Heavy Metal you may jump around, for R & B you may step back and forth to the rhythm.

3. Now rate <u>How you Feel</u> again on a scale from 0-10:

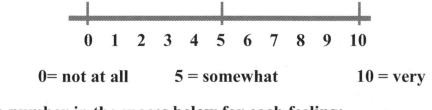

0= not at all   5 = somewhat   10 = very

Write a number in the spaces below for each feeling:

Happy _____   Sad _____   Full of Energy _____   Sluggish _____

Was there a change in your rating? _____
Why do you think there was or wasn't a change in your rating?

PART THREE:

STEPS to a Healthier You

Goals:

- Introduce the word STEPS (which stands for: set a goal, try to eat healthier, positive self- talk, and stay with it) to help guide the family to a healthier lifestyle.
- Set a target goal for eating and exercise.
- Set smaller steps to achieve the eating and exercise goals.
- Use imagery to visualize successful achievement of goals.
- Use of food and exercise diaries to help monitor progress.
- Introduce the use of positive affirmations to improve motivation.
- Introduce the use of a weekly check in with a parent/guardian to help keep the child motivated.
- Introduce rewards for achieving goals.

After Jasmine looked at all of the eating & exercise information Dr. G. had given her. She did not know where to start on her road to healthier eating. Dr. G. told her about the <u>STEPS</u> to living a healthier life style.

S = Set a goal or target

T = Try eating healthier foods

E = Exercise

P = Positive Self Talk

S = Stay with it!

Dr. G. taught Jasmine some important lessons. He said that when you go on a trip and use a GPS you have to know your destination or else the GPS will not know where to take you. The same is true for living a healthier life style; you have to know your goal or target then you can take the necessary steps to reach it.

Below is Jasmine's target/goal for Eating:

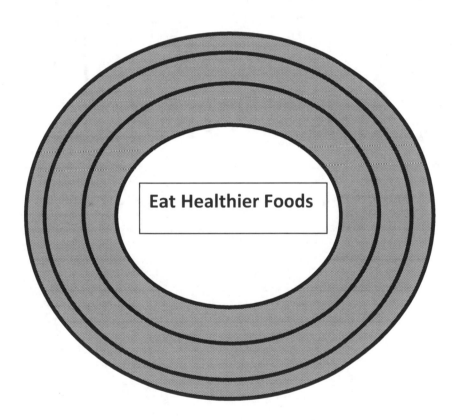

Eat Healthier Foods

Below write your target/goal for Eating:

(Color your target)

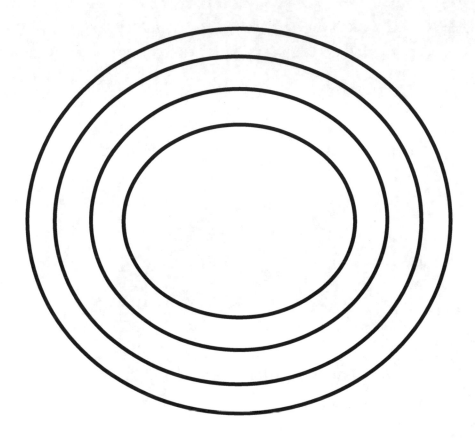

Jasmine told Dr. G. that she saw her goal but that it seemed so far away. How would she ever get there? Dr. G. told her to set a series of smaller goals on the way to her larger goal and then reward herself when she achieved them by telling herself "good job" or doing something fun. This would make reaching her goal a lot easier and would feel less overwhelming.

Baby Steps to Jasmine's Eating Goal:

Here are Jasmine's baby **steps** to her eating goal:

Goal : Eat Healthier Foods

Make vegetables ½ of my plate

Eat more fish & less red meat

Avoid foods that list Sugar as one of the 1st 3 ingredients on the label

Eat less Fat= Eat more fat-free & low fat foods

Eat Healthy snacks like apples or carrots

Baby Steps to Your Eating Goal:

Below write the **steps** you will take to reach your eating goal:

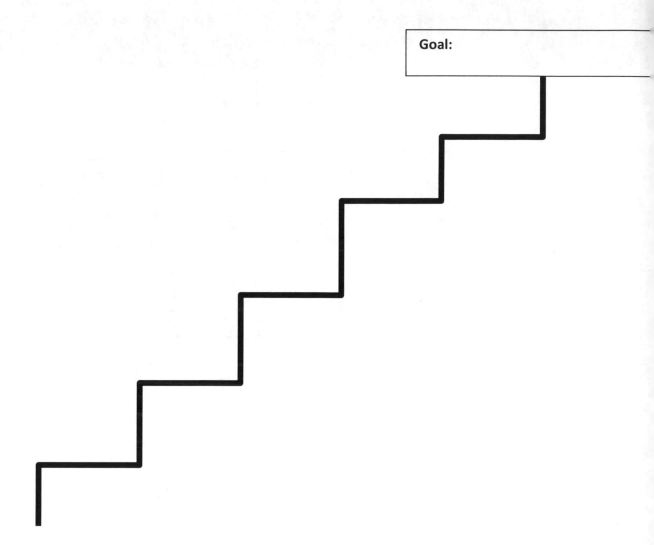

Goal:

Note: Check with your healthcare provider about your plan to eat healthier to make sure your plan is right for you and your dietary needs. Do not punish a child for not achieving their goal. Try to find out why they did not achieve it and help them make adjustments for their success.

After Jasmine wrote her baby steps to eating healthier Dr. G. told her to close her eyes and imagine herself doing each step and succeeding all the way up to her goal. This helped Jasmine see that she could do it!

Imagine Success at Each Step

Close your eyes and in as much detail as possible imagine yourself doing each baby step and being successful.

How do you feel? _____
(Write or Draw your answer)

Jasmine kept track of her progress using a food diary. She later compared it to the food dairy that she kept before she set her healthy eating goals. You can too.

My Food Diary

(*Before using make copies of this form for future weeks)

Day of Week	Time of Day	What You Ate	How Much or How Many?

How many times did you eat between meals? _____

Jasmine knew from the story The Tale of Two Athletes: The Story of Jumper and The Thumper that eating healthier alone would not help her reach her goal of living a healthier lifestyle. She would also have to exercise. Dr. G. helped her set an exercise target/goal.

Below is Jasmine's target/goal for Exercise:

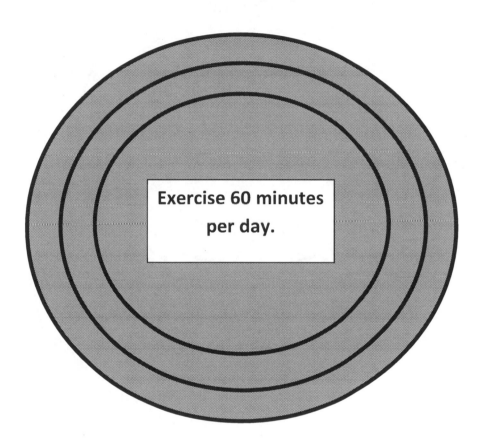

Exercise 60 minutes per day.

Below write your target/goal for Exercise:

(Color your target)

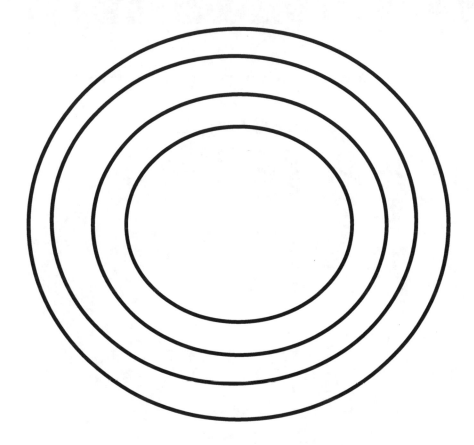

Baby Steps to Jasmine's Exercise Goal:

Here are Jasmine's baby **steps** to her exercise goal:

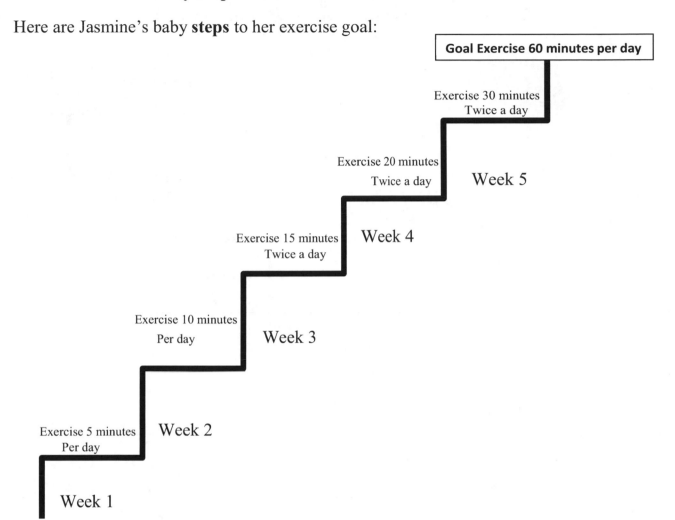

Baby Steps to Your Exercise Goal

Below write the **steps** you will take to reach your exercise goal:

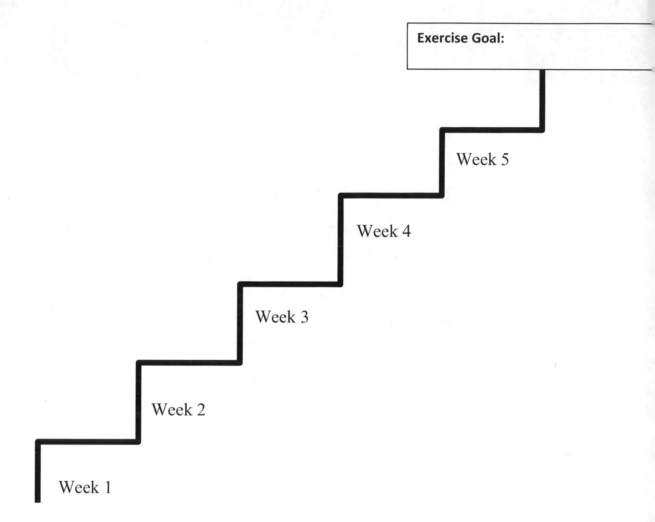

Exercise Goal:

Week 5

Week 4

Week 3

Week 2

Week 1

*Tip: Remember to set small goals that you can reach, then once you reach the small goal, change it to a harder goal to challenge yourself. For example, if you normally exercised 0 hours per week, you don't want to set a goal of 60 minutes per day. Try starting with 5 minutes per day, or 5 minutes 3 times a week. When you reach that goal, set a new one for the next week. For example, exercising 10 minutes a day and so on. Don't forget to check with your doctor to set goals that are appropriate for you. Do not punish a child for not achieving their goal. Try to find out why they did not achieve it and help them make adjustments for their success.

After Jasmine wrote her baby steps to increasing her physical activity, Dr. G. told Jasmine to close her eyes and imagine herself doing each step and succeeding all the way up to her goal.

Imagine Success at Each Step

Close your eyes and in as much detail as possible imagine yourself doing each baby step and being successful.

How do you feel? _____

(Write or Draw your answer)

Jasmine kept track of her progress with a physical activity diary. She compared it to the physical activity diary she did before she set her goal. You can too.

My Physical Activity Diary

(*Before using make copies of this form for future weeks)

Day of Week	Time of Day	Activity	Duration

Dr. G. told Jasmine that staying positive would help her along the way. He told her to focus on what she could do as opposed to what she couldn't. He told Jasmine to use Positive Affirmations such as "I can do it" to help her along the way. Jasmine put positive affirmations on an index card on her mirror and read them each morning to begin her day of living healthier.

These are the things Jasmine said to herself to help her along the way:

Circle three that you like

I Can Do It	Never give up	I Can Reach My Goal
I Am Doing My Best	I Am On My Way	I Am a Winner
I Am Healthy	I Can Overcome Challenges	I am Stronger Everyday
I Take Good Care of Myself	I Enjoy Being Positive	I Enjoy Exercising
I Enjoy Eating Healthy Foods	I Love Being Healthy	I Am Strong
I Believe In Myself And My Abilities		

Write Your Own Positive Affirmations:

_____

_____

_____

*Tip: _Put positive affirmations on an index card and carry it with you or put them on an index card on your mirror at home._

Jasmine needed a little help to keep her motivated. Dr. G. suggested that she do a weekly check in with her mother. During this time she could talk about her feelings and if she reached her goal for the week. If she reached her goal for the week then she could chose a reward from the reward menu.

Jasmine's Weekly Check In Sheet

Goal for the Week	Was Goal Met? (write yes or no)	Feelings for the Week
Exercise 5 minutes per day	Yes	Frustrated, Happy

Jasmine's Reward Menu
(Choose a weekly reward from the menu below)

Game time with parent/guardian   15 minutes extra time before bed

A trip to the park   Take a walk with family

Bike ride with parent/guardian   Have a friend come over

Have a friend sleep over   A trip to the dollar store for toy

Rent a movie   Bike ride with a friend

My Weekly Check In Sheet (Teen/Adult)

(*Before using make copies of this form for future weeks)

Directions: at the beginning of each week write down your weekly goal on this sheet. Keep track of how you are doing on the food diary and exercise diary. At the end of the week write in whether or not the goal was met. If the goal was met then pick a reward from the menu below. (<u>Note:</u> teens can start with a weekly reward or a daily reward [see next page] and then graduate to weekly rewards).

Goal for the Week	Was Goal Met? (write yes or no)	Feelings for the Week

My Reward Menu

(Choose a weekly reward from the menu below)

Game time with parent/guardian   15 minutes extra time before bed

A trip to the park   Take a walk with family

Bike ride with parent/guardian   Have a friend come over

Have a friend sleep over   A trip to the dollar store for toy

Rent a movie   Bike ride with a friend

Write In your own reward: _____

*Remember praise is always the best reward. Also, schedule a regular check in with your healthcare provider. Do not punish a child for not achieving their goal. Try to find out why they did not achieve it and help them make adjustments for their success.

Sample: **Weekly Check In Sheet (Younger Children)**

Directions: at the beginning of each week write down your daily and weekly goal on this sheet. Keep track of how you are doing on the food diary and exercise diary. At the end of each day place a check or a sticker for the day if the daily goal was met. If the daily goal was met then the child can pick a daily reward from the menu below. At the end of the week write the number of days the daily goal was met. If the weekly goal was met then pick a reward from the menu below.(Note: Younger children often need a daily and a weekly reward).

Goal for the day (eating): Make ½ my plate vegetables

Goal for the week (eating) : Have at least 4 checks for the week (I made ½ of my plate vegetables for at least 4 days)

Mon.	Tues.	Wed.	Thurs.	Fri.	Sat.	Sun.	Total
✔	✔			✔	✔		4

Note: This child will receive a daily reward on Mon., Tues., Fri. and Sat. and a weekly reward.

Goal for the day (exercise): Exercise at least 15 minutes per day

Goal for the week (exercise): Have at least 5 checks for the week (I exercised 15 minutes per day for at least 5 days)

Mon.	Tues.	Wed.	Thurs.	Fri.	Sat.	Sun.	Total
✔		✔	✔	✔	✔		5

Note: This child will receive a daily reward on Mon., Wed., Thurs., Fri., and Sat. and a weekly reward.

My Reward Menu (Choose a daily/weekly reward from the menu below):

Daily Rewards
Game time with parent/guardian

15 minutes extra time before bed

Bike ride with parent/guardian

Take a walk with family

Watch a movie

Weekly Rewards
A trip to the park

Have a friend come over

Have a friend sleep over

A trip to the dollar store for toy

Bike ride with a friend

My Weekly Check In Sheet (Younger Children)
(*Before using make copies of this form for future weeks)

Directions: at the beginning of each week write down your daily and weekly goal on this sheet. Keep track of how you are doing on the food diary and exercise diary. At the end of each day place a check or day if the daily goal was met. If the daily goal was met then the child can pick a daily reward from the menu below. At the end of the week write the number of days the daily goal was met. If the weekly goal was met then pick a reward from the menu below.(Note: Younger children often need a daily and a weekly reward. A discussion about their feelings can also be held daily).

Goal for the day (Eating): _____

Goal for the week(Eating): _____

Mon.	Tues.	Wed.	Thurs.	Fri.	Sat.	Sun.	Total

Goal for the day (Exercise): _____

Goal for the week (Exercise): _____

Mon.	Tues.	Wed.	Thurs.	Fri.	Sat.	Sun.	Total

My Reward Menu (Choose a daily/weekly reward from the menu below):

Daily Rewards	Weekly Rewards
Game time with parent/guardian	A trip to the park
15 minutes extra time before bed	Have a friend come over
Bike ride with parent/guardian	Have a friend sleep over
Take a walk with family	A trip to the dollar store for toy
Watch a movie	Bike ride with a friend

Write Your own reward _____

*Remember praise is always the best reward. Daily rewards are typically not as large as the weekly reward. Do not punish a child for not achieving their goal. Try to find out why they did not achieve it and help them make adjustments for their success. Also, schedule a regular check in with your healthcare provider.

_____

PART FOUR:
Handling Setbacks/Staying With It

Goals:

- Help the child identify potential "bumps in the road" or setbacks.
- Help the child identify ways to overcome setbacks
- Encourage staying with the new healthier life style and not giving up.

Dr. G. told Jasmine to think about her target as a goal at the end of a road. There may be bumps in the road along the way. These are things that you need to overcome to reach your goal. For Jasmine chocolate bars and fried chicken were her bumps in the road. What are your bumps in the road?

Draw or write your bumps in the road below:

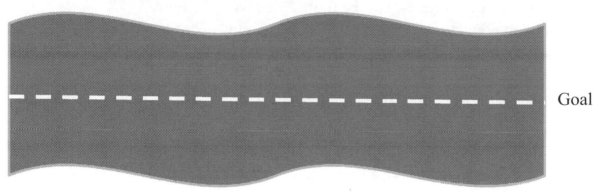

Goal

What Will You Do To Overcome Them?
(Circle the ones you will try)

Try a food alternative from the food list	Imagine yourself jumping over the bump & succeeding	Positive Self-Talk "I Can Do It"
Focus on the goal	Remove the obstacle	Talk to a dietician
Talk to a counselor or teacher	Talk to a parent or guardian	Talk to a Friend

Write your own: _____

Although Jasmine had bumps in the road/setbacks she reached her goals. Dr. G. taught Jasmine some things to help her "stay with it" and not give up.

Dr. G's Tips for Staying With It & Not Giving Up

- Don't get stuck in the setbacks/potholes. It is over (in the past) so move on. You can't change the past but you can learn from it and you can do something about the present and the future. You have the Power.
- Learning something new takes practice. For example, when a baby takes its first steps it is likely to fall. It gets back up and tries again. That is how most new things are learned and mastered.
- The more you do something the more it becomes like a habit. The more you exercise and eat healthy foods the more it will become normal for you to do so.
- It is easier to eat healthy and exercise if your whole family does it with you.
- Having an exercise buddy helps keep you motivated.
- Some people give up after the first few weigh ins because they do not notice any more weight loss. Remember muscle weighs more than fat. Go by how you feel and how your clothes fit.
- Focus on what you have achieved so far to help you move forward.

PART FIVE:
Celebrating a Healthier You

Goals:

- **Fill out and decorate a completion certificate**
- **Name your character**
- **Tell your story**

When Jasmine met her goals Dr. G. and her mother gave her a certificate. Dr. G. told her that now she was one of the characters in *The Tale of Two Athletes: The Story of Jumper and The Thumper*. Jasmine wrote the name of her character on her certificate.

CERTIFICATE OF ACHIEVEMENT

I CELEBRATE A HEALTHIER ME

This is to certify that _____ Jasmine _____

Has completed *The Tale of Two Athletes: The Story of Jumper and The Thumper Workbook* **and has met her goals toward becoming healthier.**

The new character's name is ____ **The Runner** _____

(Write the Name of the New character in our story)

Parent/Guardian Signature _____ *Mommy* _____

Date _____ June 17, 2011 _____

CERTIFICATE OF ACHIEVEMENT
I CELEBRATE A HEALTHIER ME

This is to certify that _____

Has completed *The Tale of Two Athletes: The Story of Jumper and The Thumper Workbook* **and has met his/her goals toward becoming healthier.**

The new character's name is _____

(*Write the Name of the New character in our story*)

Parent/Guardian Signature _____

Date _____

Color your certificate to make it your own.

Then Dr. G. said something very special. He said "Now it is time to tell your story. I hope it has a Happy Ending".

Write or Draw Your Character's Story in the Space Below
(Tell about your journey from being unhealthy to being healthier and how you overcame bumps in the road. How will your story end?)

Now that you have told your story, ask your parent/guardian to Log on to our Facebook page at www.Facebook.com/JumperandTheThumper to sign in and name your character. Also, every time you tell the story of Jumper and The Thumper let us know what state you were in. We hope to get the story told to families across the U.S. and beyond!

APPENDIX A:

Helpful Websites

http://apps.nccd.cdc.gov/dnpabmi/-
This website has a child and adolescent Body Mass Index (BMI) calculator.

www.aap.org/obesity/index.html
This is the American Academy of Pediatrics website which has a lot of useful information and resources about childhood obesity.

www.bam.gov/index.html
Body and Mind website by the CDC. This is a child friendly website where children can make their own customized fitness and activity calendars, print out recipes, and more.

www.cdc.gov/healthyweight/children/index.html
Has tips for parents to help their children maintain a healthy weight. Has a useful resource list.

www.cdc.gov/physicalactivity
Has guidelines and suggestions for physical activity for children.

www.choosemyplate.gov
Has tips on choosing healthier foods for your plate, has a BMI calculator, sample menus, and tips for eating healthy when eating out. It also has a chart that shows the amount of empty calories in some foods (for example 1 cup of vanilla ice cream has 210 empty calories vs. 1 cup yogurt has 119 empty calories).

www.dietaryguidelines.gov
Has guidelines for dietary requirements for children and adults.

www.fda.gov
Has information on food labels and healthy eating.

www.freeprintablebehaviorcharts.com
Has great healthy eating and exercise charts.

www.fruitsandveggiesmatter.gov
Great interactive website for parents to use with their children to encourage eating more and trying new fruits and vegetables- the website has a huge list of fruits and vegetables and the child picks one and then the website provides healthy recipes for that fruit or vegetable. Families can make their own cookbook of their favorite recipes. There is an interactive chose my plate where kids can drag food items to their plate and the website gives calorie and fat information. This website has great tips and recipes.

www.health.gov/dietaryguidelines/2010.asp
Has dietary guidelines.

www.healthychildren.org
Has great information for children and parents about eating healthier.

http://hp2010.nhlbihin.net/healthyeating/recipeslist
Has healthy recipes.

www.letsmove.gov
Michelle Obama's program for healthy eating and exercise. Has a host of information to help parents, kids, and communities get moving to prevent obesity.

www.nhlbi.nih.gov
Has a free online child tested healthy cookbook entitled *Deliciously Healthy Family Meals.*

www.nutrition.gov
Has BMI calculator and links to energy expenditure and calorie target calculators. These tell you how many calories your body burns in its normal functioning so you can make a plan that is right for you.

www.surgeongeneral.gov/obesityprevention/
Has recommendations for parents, teachers, and communities to help prevent obesity.

www.teamnutrition.usda.gov/library.html
Has very useful resources such as: healthy food buying guide, recipes, and posters.

www.wecan.nhlbi.nih.gov
Has great information for parents and communities to help get children/families healthier.

Recommended Reading

Dietz, William and Stern L. (Eds.) (2011). .*Nutrition: What Every Parent Needs to Know.* American Academy of Pediatrics.

Gavin, M.I., Dowshen, S.A., and Ezenberg, N. (Eds.) (2004). *Fit Kids: A Practical* Guide to *Raising Healthy and Active Children from Birth to Teens.* New York: DK Publishing.

Hassink, Sandra (Ed). (2006) *A Parent's Guide to Childhood Obesity: A Road Map to Health.* American Academy of Pediatrics.

Hoffman, J. & Salerno J. (2012). *The Weight of a Nation: To Win We Have to Lose.* New York: St. Martin's Press.

Schor, Edward L. (Ed.). (1999). *Caring for Your School Age Child: Ages 5 to 12.* American Academy of Pediatrics. NY: Bantam Books.

References

American Academy of Pediatrics. (2012, March 7). *Promoting Physical Activity as a Way of Life.* Retrieved from http://www.Healthy Children.org.

American Heart Association.(n.d.). *Monounsaturated Fats.* Retrieved March 7, 2012 from http://www.heart.org/HEARTORG/GettingHealthy/FatsAndOils/Fats101/Monounsaturated-Fats_UCM_301460_Article.jsp#.T1eZrzFumSo.

Centers for Disease Control and Prevention.(n.d.). *Tips for Parents-Ideas to Help Children Maintain a Healthy Weight.* Retrieved September 10, 2011 from http://www.cdc.gov/healthyweight/children/index.html.

Centers for Disease Control and Prevention. (2011, Nov. 9). *How Much Physical Activity Do Children Need?* Physical Activity for Everyone: Guidelines: Children. Retrieved from http://www.cdc.gov/physicalactivity/everyone/guidelines/children.html.

National Institute of Health. (n.d.). *Low-Calorie, Lower-Fat Alternative Foods.* National Heart Lung and Blood Institute. Retrieved December 16, 2011 from http://www.nhlbi.nih.gov/health/public/heart/obesity/lose_wt/lcal_fat.htm.

National Institute of Health. (2011, August). *Balanced Energy In: Smart Food Shopping.* National Heart Lung and Blood Institute. Retrieved from www.nhlbi.nih.gov/health/public/heart/obsesity/wecan/eat-right/smart.

Sansone, Arricca.(2012, Jan.4). *Trying to lose weight? 50 Delicious (& Healthy) Foods and Drinks that Fill You Up.* Retrieved from http://www.ivillage.com/trying-lose-weight-50-delicious-and-healthy-foods-and-drinks-fill-you/4-b-415468.

Schor, Edward L. (Ed.). (1999). *Caring for Your School Age Child: Ages 5 to 12.* American Academy of Pediatrics. NY: Bantam Books.

U.S. Department of Agriculture and U.S. Department of Health and Human Services.(2010). *Dietary Guidelines for Americans, 2010, 7th Edition.* Washington, D.C. U.S. Government Printing Office.

U.S. Department of Health and Human Services.(n.d.). *Childhood Obesity.* Retrieved September 10, 2011 from http://aspe.hhs.gov/health/reports/child_obesity/.

U.S. Department of Health and Human Services (2001). *The Surgeon General's call to action to prevent and decrease overweight and obesity.* [Rockville, MD]: U.S. Department of Health and Human Services, Public Health Service, Office of the Surgeon General. Available from: U.S. GPO, Washington.

Whitehouse Task Force on Childhood Obesity Report to the President (2010, May). *Solving the Problem of Childhood Obesity Within a Generation.*